ROSALIND FRANKLIN

Unlocking DNA

Megan Borgert-Spaniol

Checkerboard Library

An Imprint of Abdo Publishing
abdopublishing.com

abdopublishing.com

Published by Abdo Publishing, a division of ABDO, PO Box 398166, Minneapolis, Minnesota 55439. Copyright © 2018 by Abdo Consulting Group, Inc. International copyrights reserved in all countries. No part of this book may be reproduced in any form without written permission from the publisher. Checkerboard Library™ is a trademark and logo of Abdo Publishing.

Printed in the United States of America, North Mankato, Minnesota
102017
012018

THIS BOOK CONTAINS
RECYCLED MATERIALS

Design: Emily O'Malley, Mighty Media, Inc.
Production: Mighty Media, Inc.
Editor: Liz Salzmann
Cover Photograph: Alamy
Interior Photographs: Alamy, pp. 9, 13, 17, 19, 21, 25; Christian Lüts/Flickr, p. 5; Library of Congress, p. 7; Shutterstock, pp. 15, 23, 27, 28 (right), 29 (left and right); Wikimedia Commons, pp. 10, 28 (left)

Publisher's Cataloging-in-Publication Data

Names: Borgert-Spaniol, Megan, author.
Title: Rosalind Franklin: unlocking DNA / by Megan Borgert-Spaniol.
Other titles: Unlocking DNA
Description: Minneapolis, Minnesota : Abdo Publishing, 2018. | Series: STEM superstar women | Includes online resources and index.
Identifiers: LCCN 2017944051 | ISBN 9781532112799 (lib.bdg.) | ISBN 9781532150517 (ebook)
Subjects: LCSH: Franklin, Rosalind, 1920-1958--Juvenile literature. | Women molecular biologists--
    Juvenile literature. | DNA--Juvenile literature.
Classification: DDC 572.809 [B]--dc23
LC record available at https://lccn.loc.gov/2017944051

CONTENTS

ROSALIND FRANKLIN

Rosalind Franklin was a brilliant **chemist** from England. She conducted many important experiments and studies. Many of Franklin's findings are still used today.

During **World War II**, Franklin studied coal and carbon. Her later research on plant viruses led the way to understanding **viral infections**. And she is best remembered for her experiments on **DNA** structure. This work opened the door to new studies in **genetics**.

Franklin's scientific training influenced every part of her life. This sometimes upset her father. Their family was Jewish, and he believed she was more committed to

> "Science and everyday life cannot and should not be separated."
>
> –Rosalind Franklin

Franklin is a well-known figure in the United Kingdom today. There is even a historical marker where she lived in the 1950s.

science than religion. Franklin respectfully defended her views. She believed in doing her best to be successful, help others, and improve the world. That is what faith meant to her. And it was through science that Franklin would make her mark.

2

LONDON UPBRINGING

Rosalind Elsie Franklin was born on July 25, 1920. She grew up in a prominent, wealthy family in London, England. Her father, Ellis Franklin, worked at a bank. Her mother, Muriel, did charity work in the community. Rosalind had three brothers and a sister.

Rosalind's parents wanted all their children to have a good education. Rosalind and her brothers and sister attended private schools growing up. Rosalind loved learning and asking questions. She enjoyed doing arithmetic and building things. She also liked to tease her brothers. But Rosalind also suffered from several illnesses as a child. Her parents made her rest when she was sick. She hated being stuck in bed while her brothers were playing.

When Rosalind was nine, her parents sent her to Lindores School for Young Ladies. This school was on the coast of England. Rosalind's parents believed the

Rosalind's great uncle, Sir Herbert Samuel, served in the British government for more than 30 years. He worked to create the state of Israel.

fresh ocean air would improve her health. Rosalind was homesick, but she enjoyed her classes. She focused her energy on her studies.

3

ST. PAUL'S GIRLS' SCHOOL

Rosalind spent two years at Lindores. She returned home in 1931 and began attending St. Paul's Girls' School. It was one of the only girls' schools in London that taught **physics** and **chemistry**. The classes were challenging. The students were encouraged to pursue higher education and professional careers.

Rosalind had shown an early interest in math and science. At St. Paul's, she fell in love with physics and chemistry. She was drawn to their use of **logic** and experiments. She also liked that she could work alone in these subjects. When Rosalind was 15 years old, she knew she wanted to be a scientist.

At 17 years old, Rosalind was ready for a higher level of education. She wanted to study at the University of Cambridge. But first she had to take entrance tests in physics and chemistry. Rosalind was nervous that

Rosalind had strong language skills. She could speak English, French, Italian, and German!

Newnham College was established in 1871. It is still a women's college today.

In the 1930s, **Nazi** forces took over Germany. Thousands of Jewish **refugees** were fleeing to England. Many of them were children without a place to stay. The Franklins worked hard to find housing for the children. They even took two refugees into their home.

she had not done well. But she passed both tests. She did particularly well on the **chemistry** test. In fact, she received the highest score of all the students who had taken it!

At the time, Cambridge had two women's colleges. They were Girton College and Newnham College. Both schools accepted Rosalind. She decided to attend Newnham.

Rosalind's father would have preferred that she pursue more traditional interests for women. These included teaching and volunteering in the community. But he knew that she had made up her mind to study science. Rosalind wanted to leave St. Paul's a year early so she could begin her college studies. Her parents supported her decision. In 1938, Rosalind left London for Cambridge.

4

AWAY TO CAMBRIDGE

Cambridge had mostly male students while Franklin studied there. At the time, female students were not considered full members of the university. This meant they could not graduate with full degrees like their male peers.

Franklin worked hard in the face of her school's unfair practices. Her focus was physical **chemistry**. This branch of chemistry studies atoms and molecules. It also studies chemical **reactions**. When Franklin wasn't studying, she played **field hockey** and tennis and went on long bike trips. She also wrote home often.

WARTIME AT CAMBRIDGE

World War II broke out before Franklin graduated from college. Her father wanted her to leave school and work for the war effort. Franklin chose to stay at Newnham. But she still did her part to help. She gave her **scholarships** to Jewish **refugees**. Later, she volunteered to help people find shelter during bombings.

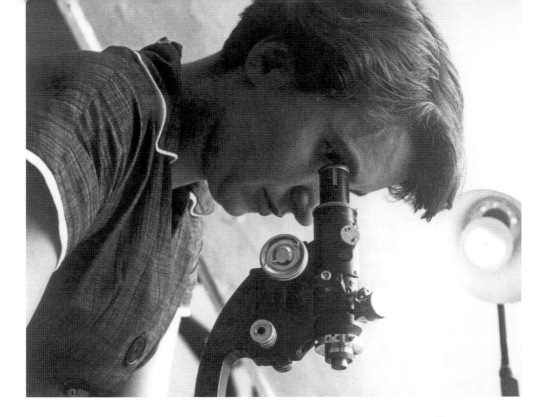

During her time at Cambridge, Franklin was known for working hard and setting high standards and goals for herself.

Franklin graduated from Newnham College in 1941. The school then offered her a research job. Franklin began her research under the direction of **chemist** Ronald Norrish. But the two did not get along.

By 1942, Franklin wanted to leave Newnham. Also, **World War II** was going on. Franklin wanted to help the war effort. That year, she got the opportunity to do both.

5

WARTIME RESEARCH

During **World War II**, German planes dropped bombs over England. People there wore gas masks so they wouldn't breathe in harmful chemicals from German bombs. Gas mask filters were made with **charcoal** that could absorb the chemicals.

At the time, the British Coal Utilization Research Association (BCURA) was doing research on coal. It wanted to find ways to improve coal's use in gas masks. In 1942, Franklin was invited to assist in BCURA's research. She worked to figure out why certain coals could absorb gas or water better than others. Coal is made up mainly of carbon. Franklin studied the structures of coal and carbon and how heat and pressure affect them.

Before she was 26, Franklin had published five papers on her experiments at BCURA. Her research on the structure of coal was considered groundbreaking.

Everyone in England was issued a gas mask by the government. Millions of masks were issued by 1940.

It contributed to the development of carbon fiber, a material used in cars and airplanes. It also earned her a **PhD** from the University of Cambridge in 1945.

6

A NEW LIFE IN PARIS

Shortly after the war ended in 1945, Franklin left BCURA. She was offered a research position in France. In February 1947, Franklin moved to Paris to continue her carbon research at a government laboratory. There, lab director Jacques Mering taught Franklin about **X-ray crystallography**. This method allowed scientists to study the structure of atoms and molecules.

Franklin became an expert in X-ray crystallography. She used it to show the structure of substances such as carbon, coal, and clay. Franklin continued to publish

UNDERSTANDING ATOMS

In 1912, scientists discovered that **X-rays** could reveal the structure of atoms in a crystal. As X-rays move through the crystal, they strike and bounce off the crystal's atoms. The X-rays then create a pattern on film. Scientists study the pattern to determine the structure of the atoms.

In Paris, Franklin learned much about French cooking and fashion.

papers on her research. She started speaking at scientific conferences. Franklin enjoyed the lively discussions among her friends and coworkers. She also felt respected as a woman in science.

However, exciting research was happening in London. Scientists were beginning to use **X-ray crystallography** to study living organisms. In 1950, she was offered a position at King's College in London. Franklin was sad to leave Paris but ready for a new stage in her career.

7

X-RAYS AND DNA

Franklin began her research at King's College in 1951. Her job was to study animal **DNA** using **X-ray crystallography**. A man named Maurice Wilkins was also doing **X-ray** research there. Wilkins was led to believe Franklin would be assisting him in DNA work. But Franklin was told she would be in charge of this research. Because of this misunderstanding, the two did not get along. They often worked separately.

At the time, scientists knew that DNA carried **genetic** information. But they didn't know how genes were passed on. They needed to understand more about the structure of DNA. Franklin and Wilkins were on the path toward this discovery. But they were not the only ones. Scientists James Watson and Francis Crick were doing similar research at Cambridge. Both teams wanted to be the first to discover the structure of DNA.

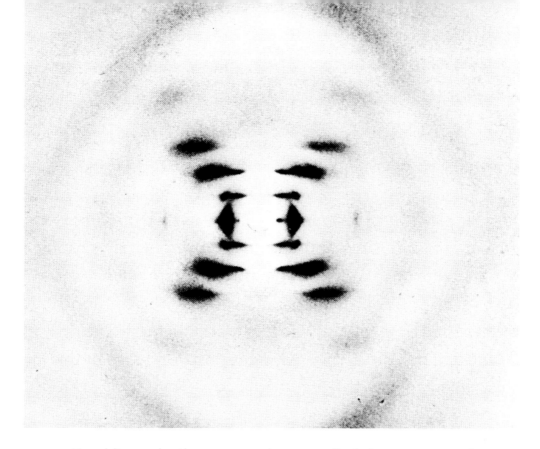

Franklin and other researchers studied the patterns of spots and bands in Photo 51. The cross of the bands shows the helix structure of DNA.

Franklin was making progress in her research. She discovered she could change the form of **DNA** by wetting it. Later, she used **X-rays** to take a photo of this DNA form. It was the clearest image of DNA structure yet. Franklin called it Photo 51.

8

THE DNA RACE

Back at Cambridge, Watson and Crick were working to build a model of **DNA** structure. They weren't doing experiments or taking **X-ray** photos. Instead, they were using studies shared by other scientists to build cardboard models of DNA. One of those scientists was Wilkins. Franklin didn't know Wilkins was giving information to Watson and Crick.

Watson and Crick were getting closer to their goal. Then, in early 1953, Wilkins showed Watson Franklin's Photo 51. Watson was shocked. The photo clearly showed the **helix** shape of the DNA. Soon after, Watson and Crick were able to get an unpublished report of Franklin's latest findings. After piecing together more research and educated guesses, the two men completed their model.

At King's College, Franklin was close to solving the structure of DNA herself. She had a paper prepared for publication. Then, news arrived that Watson and Crick had completed the model.

Nobody knew that Watson and Crick had based their model on Franklin's work. Franklin herself assumed that they made the discovery on their own. She never found out that Watson and Crick had used her findings to win the **DNA** race.

Watson (*left*) and Crick (*right*) met at the Cavendish Laboratory at Cambridge. Their work with DNA was considered one of the most important scientific discoveries of the twentieth century.

9
UNDERSTANDING VIRUSES

Even before completing the work on **DNA** structure, Franklin had decided to leave the lab at King's College. It was not an encouraging workplace for female scientists. Franklin felt alone and unhappy there. In March 1953, she took a job at Birkbeck College in London.

Birkbeck was the change that Franklin needed. She respected the scientists she worked with and they respected her. The team at Birkbeck was doing research on viruses. They were studying the structure of viruses to find out how viruses cause disease. Franklin used **X-ray crystallography** to study a plant virus called the Tobacco Mosaic Virus (TMV).

In 1955, American scientist Don Caspar joined the team. Caspar and Franklin used a new method to take clearer **X-ray** photos. Together, they discovered how the TMV reproduces. Franklin started receiving more recognition

The tobacco mosaic virus can infect many kinds of plants. The most common symptom is yellow spots or streaks on leaves.

for her work. She was invited to give talks and attend scientific conferences in Europe and the United States.

During her second US tour in 1956, Franklin went hiking and camping on the West Coast. She fell in love with Southern California. But something else happened during this trip. Franklin began to feel sharp pains in her stomach.

10

THE FIGHT FOR TIME

Back in London, Franklin continued to experience stomach pain. She went to see a doctor. After a few tests, the doctor told her what was wrong. She had **cancer**. The cancer was likely to cut her life short. But Franklin was most concerned about the work she still wanted to do.

Franklin continued to work when she could while undergoing cancer treatment. She continued to collect data, work on projects, and write papers. She even built a model of the TMV for the upcoming Brussels World's Fair. In 1957, she started studying the structure of the polio virus.

DID YOU KNOW?

Polio is a disease that can lead to **paralysis** or death. Major **outbreaks** in 1916 and 1952 resulted in thousands of deaths. The first polio **vaccinations** were given in 1954. Today, the disease is rare in most parts of the world.

Throughout her career, Franklin published 5 papers on DNA, 19 on carbon and coal, and 21 on viruses.

In early 1958, Franklin was hopeful about her future. But at the end of March, her **cancer** got worse. She had to go to the hospital. On April 16, 1958, Franklin died at age 37.

11

A LASTING LEGACY

In 1962, Watson, Crick, and Wilkins received a **Nobel Prize** for their work. The award recognized their discoveries in the structure of **DNA**. Franklin and her work were not acknowledged.

In 1968, Watson published a book titled *The Double Helix*. It was about the race to solve the DNA model. In it, Watson revealed how he and Crick had obtained their data. Over time, more people learned the truth about

X-RAYS AND CANCER

Many experts believe Franklin's **cancer** may have resulted from her work with **X-rays**. Franklin was exposed to hours of **X-ray radiation** as she prepared samples for study. Wearing a lead apron can stop most X-ray radiation from entering the body. During Franklin's career, these aprons were just starting to be used. Some scientists at the time wore them, but Franklin and others chose not to. Today, all scientists working with X-rays wear lead aprons.

Franklin's contributions. Books, articles, and films have since told the story of Franklin's role in discovering the structure of **DNA**.

Franklin did not receive the credit she deserved while she was alive. She was one of many female scientists whose contributions were overlooked during their times. But Franklin was proud of the work she had done. And today she is remembered as the brilliant scientist who discovered the structure of DNA.

Protesters at the March for Science in California in 2017 were seen with signs honoring Franklin.

TIMELINE

1920

Rosalind Elsie Franklin is born on July 25 in London, England.

1931

Rosalind begins attending St. Paul's Girls' School in London. She takes special interest in physics and chemistry.

1938

Rosalind moves to Cambridge to study at Newnham College.

1941

Franklin graduates from Newnham College and takes a research job at the college.

1945

Franklin earns a PhD from the University of Cambridge for her research at BCURA. World War II ends.

1947 ◄

Franklin moves to Paris to continue her carbon research. She learns about X-ray crystallography.

1951 ►

Franklin begins studying DNA at King's College in London.

1953 ◄

James Watson and Francis Crick use Franklin's data to build their DNA model. Franklin starts working at Birkbeck College.

1956 ►

Franklin is diagnosed with cancer.

1958 ◄

Franklin dies on April 16 at age 37.

GLOSSARY

//

cancer—any of a group of often deadly diseases marked by harmful changes in the normal growth of cells. Cancer can spread and destroy healthy tissues and organs.

charcoal—a black material that is a form of carbon.

chemistry—a science that focuses on substances and the changes they go through. Someone who studies chemistry is a chemist.

DNA—deoxyribonucleic acid. A material in the body that helps determine what features a person will inherit.

field hockey—a game that is played on a field in which each team uses curved sticks to try to hit a ball into the opponent's goal.

genetics—a branch of biology that deals with inherited features. Something related to genetics is genetic.

helix—the spiral shape formed by a line that curves around and along a central line.

logic—the science dealing with rules of correct reasoning and with proof by reasoning.

Nazi—the political party that controlled Germany under Adolf Hitler from 1933 to 1945.

Nobel Prize—any of six annual awards given to people who have made the greatest contributions to humankind. The prizes are awarded for physics, chemistry, medicine, economics, literature, and peace.

outbreak—a sudden increase in the occurrence of illness.

paralysis—the loss of motion or feeling in a part of the body.

PhD—doctor of philosophy. Usually, this is the highest degree a student can earn in a subject.

physics—a science that studies matter and energy and how they interact.

reaction—the chemical action of two or more substances on each other. This produces at least one additional substance.

refugee—a person who flees to another country for safety and protection.

scholarship—money or aid given to help a student continue his or her studies.

vaccination—a shot given to prevent illness or disease.

viral infection—an unhealthy condition caused by a virus.

World War II—from 1939 to 1945, fought in Europe, Asia, and Africa. Great Britain, France, the United States, the Soviet Union, and their allies were on one side. Germany, Italy, Japan, and their allies were on the other side.

X-ray—a powerful, invisible light wave that can pass through solid objects.

X-ray crystallography—a way to learn about the structure of a crystal by studying how X-rays bounce off it.

X-ray radiation—energy given off by X-rays.

ONLINE RESOURCES

Booklinks
NONFICTION NETWORK
FREE! ONLINE NONFICTION RESOURCES

To learn more about Rosalind Franklin, visit **abdobooklinks.com**. These links are routinely monitored and updated to provide the most current information available.

INDEX